Pierre Bonnard in a
photograph of 1945

BONNARD

"My first memory of Bonnard is of a thin, somewhat stooped, shy and short-sighted young man. Around his cheeks curled a short brown beard. His round metal glasses were slightly rusty and typical of those worn at the end of the last century. Behind his glasses he had very deep, dark eyes."

Thadée Natanson, 1951

Bonnard's long life was outwardly as serene and uneventful as the lives of Gauguin and Van Gogh were tempestuous. He was born near Paris in Fontenay-aux-Roses on 3 October 1867 and died nearly 80 years later in his little pink house at Le Cannet on the Côte d'Azur. Although he once mingled in artistic circles, he had always lived in a discreet, reserved manner, dedicated to his work and to Marthe. For 50 years Marthe was his model, his lover and his wife, his muse and the often tyrannical companion of his solitude.

Bonnard above all seemed to want tranquillity and a simple life with few preoccupations - perhaps an inheritance from the ordered life of his father, a civil servant in the Defence Ministry. From early in his life Bonnard would seek solace in nature, with which he often felt more sympathy than with human society. As a child he was first interested in drawing and then in painting. Tradition - and faithfulness to nature - formed his early style which began to take shape when he joined the Académie Julien (an art school) in

1887 - the year before he graduated in law. It was here that he met Maurice Denis and Paul Sérusier. Sérusier had just returned from Pont-Aven in Brittany where, under Paul Gauguin's dramatic influence, he had painted *Talisman*. At the Ecole des Beaux-Arts the following year he met Vuillard and Xavier Roussel. Together they formed the Nabis group - a Hebrew word meaning "prophets" - whose style was inspired by Gauguin's use of colour and rhythmic pattern.

But Bonnard and Vuillard, who opened a studio together in

A photograph of the young Pierre Bonnard, (c. 1890).

Pigalle (a poor area of northern Paris), although both members of the Nabis group, did not abide by its rules. Bonnard's pictures were dominated by his own emotions rather than literary ideas. He was never trapped in the mystical web of Symbolism. His subject matter ranged from circus scenes (page 6) to the Parisian boulevards where lamplight shines on the passers-by in the foreground (page 8). He painted languid nudes, such as *The Lazy Girl* (page 24), domestic interiors and portraits like the one of his sister, Andrée (page 4).

Andrée married a friend of Bonnard called Claude Terrasse, who was largely responsible for

introducing Symbolism into the theatre. In 1896 Terrasse and Bonnard produced the sets and scenery for *Ubu Roi,* the extraordinary and outrageous play by Alfred Jarry at the Nouveau Théâtre.

Success for Bonnard had really come in 1891. He was commissioned to paint a poster for France-Champagne, a famous champagne house in Reims. Its unexpected success led to an introduction to Toulouse-Lautrec, who was curious to meet its young designer and who introduced him to other painters. The work also earned Bonnard his first hundred francs. It was the beginning of a

A poster by Bonnard for La Revue Blanche (1894). Paris, Musée d'Orsay.

career which was to prove financially almost as secure as his father's in the civil service, although he never made a lot of money. The France-Champagne poster, which first displayed Bonnard's genius, opened the way to the important art dealer Ambroise Vollard. Bonnard and other artists and literary figures were invited to parties in Vollard's gallery on Rue Laffitte.

At some point between 1892 and 1893 Bonnard began illustrating *Le Petit Solfège* (page 2) for his brother-in-law. He also made 20 lithographs for *Les Petites Scènes Familières.* The following year he completed a poster for *La Revue Blanche.* Bonnard was subsequently commissioned by Vollard to make engravings as illustrations for various important books. The artist illustrated books such as Paul Verlaine's *Parallèlement* (page 20), *Daphne And Chloe* by Longo Sofista, *Dingo* by Octave Mirbeau and in 1930, *Saint Monica* by Vollard himself. All his life, such illustrations were to provide an important part of his income.

In 1894, when he was 27, Bonnard met Marthe, the woman around whom his life soon began to revolve. She was 25, blue-eyed, slim and markedly attractive. She introduced herself to Bonnard under a false name. She had been christened Marie Boursin but, to fascinate the artist, she selected the name of Marthe de Melliny from a romantic novel. Bonnard only discovered the real identity of this disconcerting woman 30 years later. By then her name was no longer important, for Marthe had long since been the chief figure in both his life and art.

Such a passionate and exclusive love did not prove easy. Bonnard painted endless pictures of Marthe. He was attracted equally by her personality and her naked body. He took the greatest care to portray her at her most beautiful, even when she grew older. They married in 1925 and were scarcely ever apart.

Bonnard was always quick to justify Marthe's often eccentric behaviour on the grounds of her poor health - she was tubercular and had bouts of depression. She was also prone to extraordinary outbursts of jealousy which dismayed the artist's friends. They could not understand her efforts to hide Bonnard from the world. Such seclusion suited Bonnard.

Bonnard came to depend on Marthe, although her aggressiveness could be a burden. Some of the portraits of women that he painted, such as *Nude Against The Light* (page 20) or *Nude In The Bath* (page 24), lead one to believe that Marthe's fits of jealousy were not

The artist photographed with Marthe at Vernon in 1915

entirely groundless. He painted many resplendently sensual young women as nude studies, such as *Nude In The Mirror* (page 20), which are among the most powerfully erotic pictures of the century. Little wonder that Marthe felt jealous of his young models. He also, less contentiously, painted many marvellous landscapes such as *Landscape Of Le Cannet* (page 28), which confirmed his position as the heir of the Impressionist tradition. For this he was honoured in 1940 by being made a member of the Royal Academy in London.

Until he discovered Le Cannet most of his time was spent

in the countryside of Burgundy, the Auvergne, Provence and Normandy. Then, in 1909, he spent the summer on the Côte d'Azur. This proved to be a watershed in his life. It was here that he discovered "the sea, the yellow walls and the many-coloured reflections of the light". He described the effect of the sun as "a Mediterranean fairytale", surpassing anything that he had seen before. From that moment, he found that he was unable to live without the landscapes of the south of France.

He also travelled abroad to visit museums and study the landscape. However, when discussing the Louvre, he once said that "windows are the most beautiful thing in a museum". He visited Belgium, Holland, England, Spain, Rome, Tunisia and Algeria. In 1926 he even went to the United States to be one of the judges awarding the prestigious Carnegie prize.

When Marthe died in January 1942 Bonnard withdrew entirely into himself. His immense sense of grief and loss did not, however, stop him forging Marthe's will to make it leave everything to himself - a move which was discovered and caused a lot of trouble. Apart from two brief trips to Paris, he never again left his house so filled with memories of his life with Marthe. He died there on 23 January 1947.

A page from Bonnard's diary (December 1937)

THE CHECKED BODICE

1892 - Oil on canvas, 61 x 33 cm
Paris, Musée d'Orsay

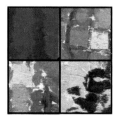

Coloured plates like these have been printed at the beginning of each commentary on the individual paintings. The aim is to reproduce the harmonies and contrasts that form the basis of the work's colour composition.
In *The Checked Bodice*, Bonnard is already using his grids - the markings that serve to order and frame the different colour zones: the browns of the background, the reddish-pink and orange checks of the bodice.

The characteristics of Bonnard's work were already evident in his first paintings, such as this portrait executed in Paris. It is a study of his sister Andrée, quite simply eating her supper. Bonnard was to make the portrayal of everyday life one of his specialities. This intimacy and a sense of secrecy character-ised the work of a group of artists who came together in the summer of 1888, among whom was Paul Sérusier. Sérusier was a young Parisian artist who had painted *Talisman* after a stimulating conver-sation with the group's master, Paul Gauguin.
"What colour is that tree?" Gauguin had asked. "Green? Well then, use the most beautiful green on your palette." "How do you see the shade?" "Blue." "Well, don't hesitate to use the bluest blue possible."
The outcome was a landscape made up of synthetic (simplified and exaggerated) forms and large areas of dazzling and yet harm-onious colours. This was the beginning of the group known as the Nabis painters - the group with which Bonnard was linked. Bon-nard was indeed to be a prophet of everyday life and the elevation of the ordinary to an idealised plane hitherto reserved for nobler topics. *The Checked Bodice* combines the warm reds and oranges of the checks with the long arabesques of the folds, blending them with the rosy face and the brown back-ground. The colours are set off by the white table cloth and the plates. His sister is holding a fork in one hand and a dog with the other.

The Checked Bodice *is a portrait of Bonnard's sister, Andrée. The painter drew his inspiration from this engraving by Utagawa Kunisada (Japanese Woman In A Checked Kimono - 1845/46), which formed part of his own extensive collection of Japanese prints. Checks often feature in Bonnard's paintings. They appear not only on clothes, but also on table cloths, carpets and other furnishings.*

*Edouard Vuillard: Marie Vuillard Writing - 1883 Oil on board, 37 x 29 cm, Paris, Private collection. Bonnard and Vuillard knew each other even before they were both members of the Nabis group. Like Bonnard, Vuillard found in simple everyday reality his true subject matter. His paintings are visions, alive with love and laden with memories.
The composition of the painting and the Japanese influence are both striking. The foreground looms large to the left, with the red of the dress standing out against the delicate swirls of the white curtain. It is as though everything is painted as part of a subtle visual and psychological game, made up of reality and memory.*

THE BAREBACK RIDER

1897 - Oil on canvas 26 x 35 cm
Aix-les-Bains, Musée des Beaux-Arts

The colours used by Bonnard in *The Bareback Rider* are basically the yellowy-white of the horse, the blueish yellow of the bands of the seats, the maroon of the actual rows and the blue-green of the spectators' silhouettes. There are no smooth colours; all the tones are ruffled with reflections to give the impression of oscillating movement.

Georges Seurat: The Circus 1890-91 - Oil on canvas 186 x 151 cm - Paris, Musée d'Orsay. Seurat's painting in some ways resembles Bonnard's, with the horse pushing out to the left of the canvas. But in Seurat's picture the detailed execution and ordered form of the characters gives a far more detached, cooler image than Bonnard's fleeting vision.

The world of the circus fascinated many artists from Degas, Toulouse-Lautrec and Seurat to Fernand Léger and Picasso in the 20th century. No doubt this was due to the acrobatic cavortings of its performers, the dazzling lights and the presence of animals - above all the danger inherent in almost every act. Everything amusing, difficult, sad - in short, all the experiences of human life - seemed magnified in a circus, as in a distorting mirror.

Its themes, which fuelled private inner fantasies and emotions, fascinated a painter like Bonnard. He captured with his colours, his composition and his overall view, one moment of this whirling universe of people, lights and colours. The white silhouette of a horse, above which a bareback rider with long legs performs her acrobatics, spins at immense speed against a background punctuated by the maroon, yellow and green bands of the seats. This gives the impression of seeing a somewhat blurred instant of action, as if in a dream or a memory. The horse has crossed the "stage" of the picture and is about to make its exit to the left, head down, its hooves raised above a blue-tinted ring (giving the illusion that the ring is covered in water not sand). The bareback rider is spread out on the horse's back, as if suspended in mid-air. Dream and reality intermingle in this vision of colour, light and movement.

Toulouse-Lautrec: Bareback Rider at Fernando's 1888 - Oil on canvas - 98 x 161 cm - Chicago, Art Institute. Comparison between Toulouse-Lautrec's work and that of Bonnard is interesting because it allows us to measure the weight and the density of the figures in the first picture to gauge the abstraction of the second. In Toulouse-Lautrec's painting, the horse is painted with a strong, solid body and the rider is firmly planted on its back. With Bonnard, the horse is a flicker of light above which the figure of the young girl vibrates.

"I always enjoy myself at the circus and, for a solitary person, it has the inestimable advantage of boasting intervals as amusing as those of a theatre are tedious. I go to the bar where clowns are drinking away."

Bonnard

MONTMARTRE

1907 - Oil on canvas, 36 x 49 cm
Washington, Phillips Collection

Grey is the dominant colour (Bonnard had probably written "cloudy weather" in his diary). The grey-blue of the moving figures, the blue of the violets, the purple of the flowers in their baskets and the dark grey - almost black - of the figure in the foreground on the right are all seen against the grey background of the street.

Day after day, Bonnard noted the weather conditions in his diary: "fine," "cloudy," "fog," "rain." He enriched these notes with sketches of little, familiar, every-day things that struck him and stuck in his memory.

For Bonnard, mundane every day activities - people coming and going - were the very essence of art. In this snapshot-like view of a part of a Montmartre street, Bonnard shows the influence of the Impressionists not only in his very softly outlined forms but, more importantly, in his choice of subject. This undramatic, every-day scene, was for him the most interesting and worthy of topics, just as it had been for the major Impressionists.

The influence of photography is also obvious in the way he has cut off the group of people on the right and the man on the left just as if he had actually taken a quick unposed photograph.

The soft grey light which envelops everything is typical of his palette at this stage, before he discovered the Mediterranean with its strong clear colours.

Above: Boulevard - 1899 Lithograph, 17 x 43 cm - Bremen, Kunsthalle. Strongly vertical lines from the street's trees give an unusually forceful framework to this street scene. Left: Place Clichy - 1912 - Oil on canvas, 139 x 205 cm - Besançon, Musée des Beaux-Arts. Another shapshot-like view, "taken" from inside a cafe.

THE BOX

1908 - Oil on canvas, 91 x 120 cm
Paris, Bernheim-Jeune Collection

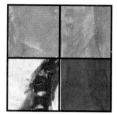

On the left is the orange of the lit-up background, the blue shades of the male figure and shade of the arms of the woman leaning on the red back of a chair. On the right in the foreground, the black and white tones of the seated woman and her standing escort emerge from the deep red background.

Bonnard here painted the Bernheim family at the Opéra. He generally disliked paintings with an obvious message or programme, preferring images that were simultaneously intimate, affectionate and sometimes also ironic. He avoided the obvious view of things, looking for emotions and leaving theories to his friends in the Nabis who talked endlessly about the works of Gauguin or of Puvis de Chavannes, the great Symbolist. He painted with very simple methods, fusing form and colour into elegant and spontaneous movements.

The originality of the composition is striking, although it picks up a constantly recurring theme in painting (one only has to look at Edouard Manet's *The Box*, or works by Degas). A woman is seated on the right; beside her an elegant gentleman is standing, whose black and white evening suit contrasts with the crimson curtains and background. On the left, the raised hangings allow a glimpse, amid orange surroundings, of two other figures: a woman with bare arms delicately leaning on the back of her armchair, and a man bathed in diffused tones. Bonnard disregarded normal perspective here; the figures on the left are larger than they ought to be. He was also totally free in this, as in later works, of the tonal rules of perspective which demanded that warm colour tones should be to the fore and cold tones to the back. He reversed that order in keeping the warmest and strongest colours (like orange) for the background.

Bonnard had the habit of going for walks with a pencil and a piece of charcoal. As is clear from this small preliminary sketch, he imbued the characters of his paintings with spontaneity and life, and managed to suggest the vibrancy of colour with pencil or charcoal.

Renoir: The First Night At The Theatre - 1876 - Oil on canvas, 65 x 50 cm - London, National Gallery. The box (a theatre within a theatre) was one of the favourite themes of the Impressionists, for they thought of the theatre as a mirror of life. In Renoir's painting, the young girl leaning out of the box is a pretext for showing the audience and the movement of the play.

The diagram shows the foreground in shadow, with the people in the background bathed in an orange glow and the woman in the front lit from a source to her left.

"When you cover a surface with colours, you must be able to
renew your work indefinitely, ceaselessly discovering new
combinations of forms and colours which respond to the demands
of the emotions."

Bonnard

AFTER THE FLOOD

1906 - Oil on canvas, 250 x 450 cm
New York, W.P.Chrysler Collection

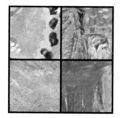

Orange is the colour of the frame, but it also infiltrates the picture, mixing with the colour of the cloaks worn by the figures to the right and the green of the field. The grey-green group of trees at the centre stand in contrast to the russet coloured animals in their shade. (Note the use of warm tones to create the shade - a departure from every tradition).

This is one of four canvases commissioned by Misia Natanson for her dining room. It is a decorative painting that was created for a practical purpose.

However, Bonnard's passionate interest in poetry, philosophy and his own strong sense of artistic freedom show through what might have been a conventional treatment of the biblical myth. Bonnard was never keen on painting any mythological or biblical subjects anyway, but he sometimes accepted such financially rewarding commissions, especially from friends like the Natansons. Thadée Natanson had asked him to design the posters for *La Revue Blanche* as early as 1894 and long remained one of his closest friends.

As he himself admitted, "I was attracted to painting and drawing for a long time before my interest became an irresistible passion. I desperately wanted to escape a monotonous way of life." Bonnard was familiar with the work of the Impressionists and with Japanese prints. He reacted against academic formality, like his Nabis contemporaries, preferring the creation of harmonious pure forms. The subject itself could become the focus of composition and colours - beneath the official or commissioned title.

Bonnard had not yet settled in the south of France. But the idyllic pastoral scene, with man and animals harmoniously united in a restored (after the Flood) nature looks forward to his later Mediterranean works, with their Arcadian undertones. His colours, however, are still fairly muted. The obvious influence is of course Gauguin, in the naked or robed figures, the general exoticism and especially the surrounding frieze which, with its monkeys and parrots, recalls Gauguin's Polynesian works.

Decorative panel - 1906 - Oil on canvas, 230 x 300 cm - Paris, M. and Mme Adrien Maeght's collection.
This panel from the same series is filled with moving animals. Bonnard arranged the composition to combine men, women, animals and plants. The painting represents the fusion of a graceful, humorous invention with the luminous force of a natural sensuality. Bonnard achieves his aim without falling into a contrived manner. It is as he wrote elsewhere in his notes: "Avoid the amusing, the picturesque and the conventional... The surface of the painting - which has its own colour and its own rules - should take precedence over the objects to become the main subject of the painting." There is a famous saying that describes Bonnard's method of working: "Painting is the transcription of the adventures of the optic nerve."

"Our life here is lonely enough and as organised as possible. Today is a bad day; snow has been falling since the morning, the maid is ill, the electricity does not work and the milk will probably not be delivered till this evening."

Bonnard

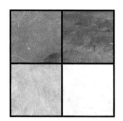

The basic colours of this large canvas are clear-cut: the reddish orange of the sky that fuses with the tones of the distant mountains, the iridescent blue of the sea tossed by waves, the violet-orange of the rocks and the bodies to the left and the white figure of the bull walking along the beach in the bright light.

The painting illustrates the myth of the Greek heroine Europa, who was kidnapped on the coast of Phoenicia by Zeus disguised as a bull. Zeus took her to Crete where she gave birth to Minos, who later became King of Crete.

At first glance this ancient myth might appear a most improbable subject for the painter of everyday life. But even Bonnard was unable to resist the contemporary demand for paintings with themes taken from myths and classical legends. Picasso, Matisse and others were painting such classical subjects at the time.

However, he approached the task of composition with complete freedom, drawing attention away from its theme to the reality of light and colour and the subtle sensuality of the female nudes. The theme became a pretext for the exultation of a kind of golden age - almost a symbol of earthly happiness.

Actually, it is a painting of a marine landscape, peopled by men, women, children and the bull, all of them seemingly part of nature itself, as Bonnard saw it in the south of France. The outline of distant mountains stands out in red and violet against the sky. The great deep blue expanse of the sea is encircled by rocks on the beach in the foreground, bathed in dazzling sunlight. The bull stands on the left, looking almost like a statue cut from chalk or salt. Two figures, the same colour as the rocks, sit on the bull. In the foreground are two

Using the decisive strokes that were typical of his style, Bonnard's sketch for The Abduction Of Europa served to establish the figures that animate the landscape of the painting. The sketch is a demonstration of Bonnard's method. Colour was the vehicle for meaning in his work, but he always used pencil sketches to establish the shapes of the figures and objects that were to be included. In the drawing the two figures and the bull are clearly defined, whilst in the painting they seem to have become part of the landscape - a chalk statue with figures that appear to be cut from pinkish rock.

strange characters - a satyr, perhaps, to judge by the hooves, though it lacks the appropriate hairy legs, and a child with bizarre features. In contrast to the beautiful bay, which is illuminated with a brilliant light, the distant landscape appears dull-coloured. The painting also reflects the culture of the time. It displays the effect that Mallarmé's poetry, with its perfectionist language, and Verlaine's, with its soft, even morbid, sensuality had on Bonnard and the artistic world at large.

Bonnard had already illustrated Verlaine's poems *Parallèlement* with some extremely sensual nudes. Now he had no intention of limiting the field of his inspiration. Here material objects are illuminated to such an extent that they seem to be set alight. The themes and the intensity of tone and colour change, but Bonnard's paintings from now on display the same pulsating tones and rich colours. Here they clearly derive from his contact with the Mediterranean world in which he had now settled.

The Gulf of Saint Tropez - 1937 - Oil on canvas, 41 x 60 cm - Albi, Musée Toulouse-Lautrec. The outline of the distant landscape stands out between the orange sky and the incredible yellow mirror of the sea. This was the year in which Bonnard wrote: "When my friends and I decided to follow and develop the theorics of the Impressionists, we sought to surpass them in their naturalistic perception of colour. Art is not Nature. We were stricter in our approach to composition. It was necessary to exploit colour to a far greater extent as a vehicle of expression. However, although our progress became increasingly rapid, society was ready to accept Cubism and Surrealism long before we had achieved our aims...."

The Beach - watercolour, 33 x 50 cm. By the time he painted this, Bonnard had already abandoned the traditional concepts of perspective, and the rule that requires the use of warm colours for the foreground and cooler ones for the background. He often preferred to paint his foregrounds in a cold tone of blue, relegating the warm orange to the far distance. By bringing forward the colours that should serve to deepen the distance and pushing back the ones that ought to stand out at the front, he tended to weaken the overall feeling of perspective.

BONNARD'S PALETTE

Bonnard was inspired by Cézanne's theory of colour: "Light is orange, shadow is blue - its complementary colour. The mezzotint (half-shade) marks the passage from orange to blue, passing through a red violet and violet blue." The colours on Bonnard's palette became almost symbols of his painting. It was as though his paintings were made of light, with blinding yellows and oranges and extraordinary new shades of violet. It was the Impressionists, following faithfully in the steps of Utamaro and the prints of other Japanese artists, that introduced violet to the palette of western painters. However, it was Bonnard who developed all the possible combinations of this colour, opening the way to another, invisible universe. It should not be forgotten that it is violet, made up of red and blue, which complements yellow. Yellow was the colour that Bonnard used above all others to express the joy and triumph of light in contrast to violet shadow.

YELLOW AND RED STILL LIFE

1931 Oil on canvas, 47 x 68 cm
Grenoble, Musée des Beaux-Arts

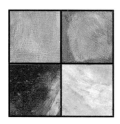

The basic colours are those of the title - the yellow of the jug and the orange of the basket harmonise with the red of the background and the colours of the sun, white and yellow. This is a shadowless table, made only of light.

About 1920 Bonnard became dissatisfied with the direction his art was taking - away from solid forms towards pure colours - and decided "to go back to school". This decision may have been partly prompted by his recent treatment of classical subjects; classical art, of course, has always emphasised form over colour. Equally, the triumphantly solid works of Paul Cézanne, who had lived in southern France not too far from Bonnard, may have been a powerful influence.

This rediscovery of form seems to have rejuvenated Bonnard as an artist. He now looked at objects with a child's fresh eye, painting with fresh, strong and simple colours but neglecting neither designs or perspective, as is evident in this still life, where vibrant colours are matched by powerfully drawn forms.

Bonnard's friend Maurice Denis' pronouncement could apply to Bonnard's work with equal justice: "Never forget that a picture, be it of a horse, a woman, a nude or anything else, is essentially a flat surface covered in colours arranged in a certain way." The secret of Bonnard's artistic language lies in this "certain way" which determines all his mature pictures. An interior, a still life, a tree in flower or a figure were basically no more than a pretext for devoting himself to his intoxication with colours and light, heedless of the subject.

Fruit Basket - 1930 - gouache on paper, 28 x 38 cm - Switzerland, Private Collection. The perspective of this basket full of fruit is outlined by traces of red in its upper corners; a snapshot effect which Bonnard achieves by contrasting the colours of the basket with the white of the table cloth.

Paul Cézanne: Still Life With Apples - 1895/8 - Oil on canvas - 68 x 98 cm - New York, Museum of Modern Art. In Cézanne's still lifes, the work is always simultaneously concerned with colour and space, tending towards an abstract style in which every day objects achieve an almost monumental importance. This also occurs in Bonnard's later paintings.

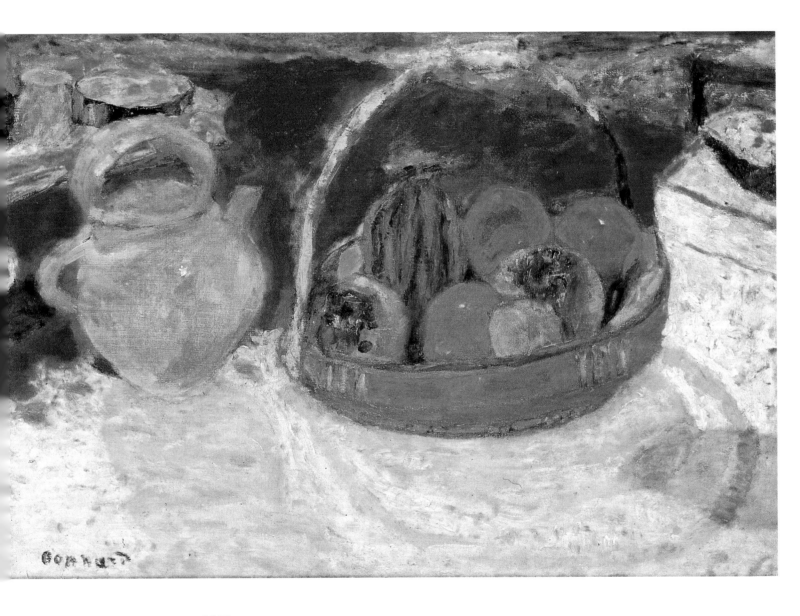

"I sent myself back to school. I wanted to forget everything I knew, I sought to learn what I had never known. I renewed my studies from first principles, starting with my ABC - and I grew to distrust everything which had so moved me, above all colour which can drive you mad..."

Bonnard

NUDE IN THE MIRROR

1931 - Oil on canvas, 153.5 x 104 cm
Venice, Museum of Modern Art, Ca' Pesaro

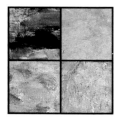

The painting plays on the contrast between the blue and the yellow, whilst the shade or rather the reflections and transparencies come from the impasto (thickly applied opaque paint) of intermediate colours, orange and violet.

Archetypal features of Bonnard's work are the mirror and the window, which allow space to be expanded. Mirrors reflect and redouble space and, above all, allow the painter to adopt a new and unexpected viewpoint. A window adds depth to a scene and expands the perspective.

These two elements have been used elsewhere by painters of all periods. Jan Van Eyck used mirrors in *The Arnolfini Marriage* in the 15th century; so did Ingres in the 19th century, (so that he could display his model in several different poses at the same time) and Manet in his *Bar At The Folies Bergère.* Windows opening out of a room figure in pictures by Renaissance masters such as Antonello da Messina or Dürer, and later the *Méninas* of Velasquez. With both of these props, therefore, Bonnard was following famous and time-honoured traditions.

This Bonnard painting is a late nude, relatively restrained compared to the lyrical eroticism of so many of his earlier studies, such as *Nude Against The Light* below; note that, as in most of Bonnard's nudes, the women are wearing high-heeled shoes, which seemed to appeal to the painter. His nudes, markedly risqué for the time, greatly appealed to contemporaries, one of the reasons he painted so many with a marked yet tender eroticism.

Ne fronce plus ces sourcils-ci,
Casta, ni cette bouche-ci,
Laisse-moi puiser tous tes baumes,
Piana, sucrés, salés, poivrés,
Et laisse-moi boire, poivrés,
Salés, sucrés, tes sacrés baumes.

Lithograph by Bonnard to illustrate Parallèlement - poems by Paul Verlaine. Bonnard found the lithograph a very agreeable medium; in it his pencil-strokes, drawn directly onto the stone, when printed merged to produce a sensual softness similar to that of oil paints.

Nude Against The Light - *1908 - Oil on canvas 124. 5 x 109 cm - Brussels, Musées Royaux des Beaux-Arts. Here, the composition is made from a slightly raised point of view. Colour fades in the light and the figure seems to dissolve against the blinding background.*

THE TABLE AND THE GARDEN

1934/35 - Oil on canvas, 127 x 135.5 cm
New York, Guggenheim Museum

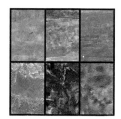

The violet shades of the table and its reflections triumphantly dominate in this interior. Its strength is increased by the blue band which is a reflection of the sky and sea outside.

There is nothing extraordinary here: a simple dining-room with a window giving onto a garden, on an ordinary sort of day - a good example of Bonnard's favourite type of subject.

It is impossible to tell, looking at this picture, if its real subject is the interior or the exterior - whether the dining-room, with the mysterious presence of the figure on the right and the table where the glasses, carafes and bowls are carefully arranged, or the garden, visible beyond the window. Perhaps it is both, with the everyday objects of the room merging with the grass, sky and sea.

Even the composition is straight forward and natural. The window is seen full face and its reflection is mirrored on the table's surface in a play of colours.

Beyond the room glints the brilliant blue sky above the cobalt blue sea - the Mediterranean with which Bonnard had fallen in love as a young man and beside which he was now living permanently. Indisputably, Bonnard wanted to reaffirm the miraculous nature of ordinary life. He succeeded due to the intensity of colour which he uses to raise this humble scene above normality making the simple objects shimmer in the brilliant light and by including the shadowy figure that melts into the background on the right.

Vuillard : Married Life - circa 1900 - Oil on canvas, 51 x 57 cm - Paris, Private collection. Vuillard like Bonnard was a painter of daily life. He painted with deep feeling objects charged with a secret meaning and significance. Everything, even the most insignificant, is painted with the same care. Such shared attitudes helped bind the lifelong friendship of the two men.

Bonnard thought of colours with great freedom and intuition. He even succeeded in turning violet into a light colour, contrasting with the deep blue of the reflection of the window on the table, the yellowy-orange of the bowls and the red of the fruits.
He cropped the silhouette (1) of a tree in flower against the background of a blue sea and sky, harmonising it with the spotted blue of the reflections and the orange of the flowers.

In the horizontal line of the window frame (2), the blue of the shade and finally the violet of the table follow the gold of the sunlight reflecting on the window. Bonnard contrasted the luminous tones of the orange pillow (3) with the dark tones of the chair against the wall. As if he wanted to transform the human figure into a mosaic (4), Bonnard placed a vase of flowers before her. The red of the flowers contrasts with the olive green of her dress.

NUDE IN THE BATH

1937 - Oil on canvas, 92 x 147 cm
Paris, Musée d'Art Moderne de la Ville de Paris

The dense drawing of the tiles on the floor and walls seems to dominate and surround Bonnard's sequence of colours: the yellow light from the window on the left is reflected on the wall, becoming warmer and more orange, approaching a shade of violet on the far right.

Marthe, his adored wife, was an inexhaustible source of inspiration for Bonnard. He studied her graceful body in every position, with different hairstyles and under different light, painting a lengthy series of nude studies of which this is one of the finest. It shows Marthe in the bath, with her naked body reflected in the bath's sides and the tiles. The tiles served as mirrors for the light reflected in the bath water and so enabled him to create splendid images, vibrant with light. He painted these images at every hour of the day - in the uncertain clearness of early morning, in full daylight, or in the violet hour of evening or the yellow glow of a soft lamp. This series dedicated to Marthe calls to mind Degas' bathing women - but that painter used several different models for his paintings, portraying them realistically. Bonnard painted idealised people and their appearance, representing only their most beautiful aspects and making them come alive through his amazing visual memory. This painting is almost an artistic fireworks display, derived from Monet's light, Renoir's sensuality and the forceful clear forms of Toulouse-Lautrec and Degas.

The Lazy Girl - circa 1899 - Oil on canvas, 92 x 108 cm Josefowitz Collection. The figure of the model is lying on an unmade double bed and the viewpoint is somewhat raised. She is illuminated by a light from the side which projects elongated shadows onto the sheet, leaving half the work in shadow. The bed adds a particularly sensual note to the scene.

This detail reveals the relation of pure colours in a mosaic of yellow and blue tiles, lighting up the tiles on the right. Bonnard here paints colour and light with vibrant splendour.

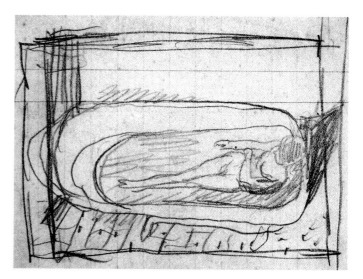

The preliminary sketch of Nude In The Bath allowed the artist to realise his composition. The choice of perspective is especially significant here, giving the impression that the woman does not know she is being watched.

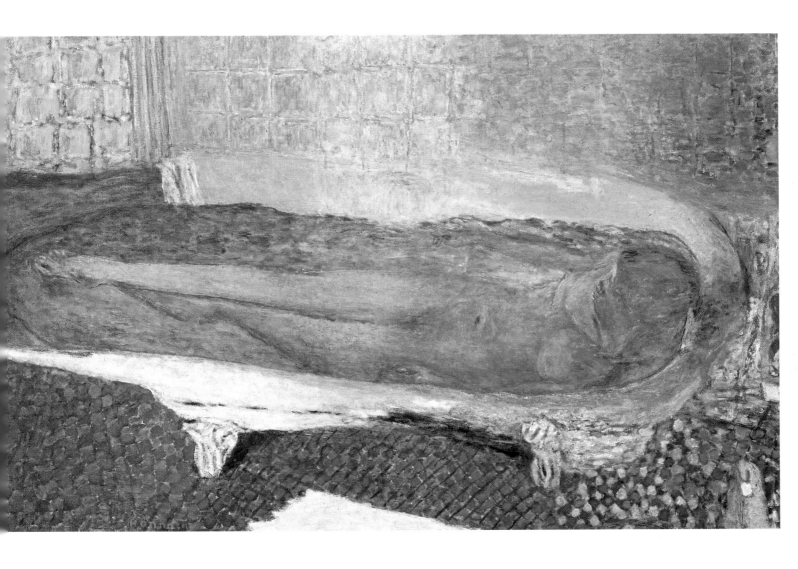

"I no longer dare get involved in really difficult themes. I don't manage to produce what I really want to. I have already been busy for six months and I have several months' more work..."

Bonnard

THE STUDIO WITH THE MIMOSA

1939/46 - Oil on canvas, 125 x 125 cm Paris,
Musée National d'Art Moderne

The colours here are archetypally mature Bonnard - warm and passionate yellows from a splash of sun. The yellow of the mimosa is set off by the frame of the window and the mixed colours of the village. There are strong geometrical bands of colour:the deep blue sky, the band of pale yellowy orange on the right, the reddish wall on the left and the horizontal splash of green at the base of the window.

Pencil study circa 1935 - Paris, Musée National d'Art Moderne. This sketch illustrates Bonnard's conviction that he should decide on the form of the subject before he allowed himself to be carried away by the joy of the colour. "I draw non-stop...a well drawn picture is half-finished."

This painting represents a summary of all the different characteristics that typified Bonnard's work. It demonstrates his particular way of conceiving and rendering space and depth with the use of grids (including the glazing bars of window frame itself) and the tilt of the balustrade in the foreground, which help give the illusion of a painting within the painting.

The mimosa is created from a shower of brush strokes, globules of light, a wall of little clusters of flowers with a luminous quality that makes them appear to represent the light itself. It is a vision that passes beyond the subject into a blaze of sunlight which seems to consume the mimosa, transforming it into an enormously powerful element in the painting. All of this is achieved through the cunning use of colour. To the left, forming the window frame, there is a great band of colour that, passing through the colours of the spectrum, (orange, yellow, green, blue), draws our attention towards the window. To the right there is a narrow orange stripe, speckled with red. These two bands of colour define the boundaries of our vision, enclosed at the top by blue and at the bottom by green. The window bars and the balustrade are a blueish white cutting dramatically across the brilliant colours and constraining the bright tones. To balance the great mass of the mimosa there is the splash of green blue of the distant houses clustered in a hollow.

The Open Window - 1921 - Oil on canvas, 118 x 96 cm - Washington, Phillips Collection. The window seems to have been thrown open onto the brightly lit space beyond. The violet tones of the interior are warmed by orange and set off by the long azure window frame. There is a vase of flowers in the foreground. To the right, a woman in a deck chair is busy playing with a cat. The trees are silhouetted against the sunny background. The mass of their foliage appears yellow-green in contrast to the light and azure-violet in the shade.

THE ALMOND TREE

1947 - Oil on canvas, 55 x 37.5 cm
Paris, Musée National d'Art Moderne

The artist used only a few vital colours to depict the almond tree exploding with flowers. He used wide white brush strokes to convey the clusters of flowers among the dark branches that stand out against the azure and violet, reds and oranges of the background.

The flowering tree seems to burst from the frame, which appears unable to contain it. Amazingly for a man who was approaching 80, Bonnard seems to have redis-covered the extraordinary emo-tional energy of a Van Gogh style of painting. The painting is a kind of vision of centrifugal force, with everything rushing outwards. In it, Bonnard has abandoned his usual grids and rectangles, filling the entire background of the canvas with a vision of absolute freedom and joy. It also demonstrates the artist's skill in extending the chro-matic range according to the spectrum, passing from yellow to violet and using wide, iridescent brush strokes. Yet it reveals as well the general lack of progress or development in Bonnard's work, which so early on found its own way and seldom strayed far from this later. This is why he has often been called the Last Impressionist, ignoring the abstract trends of so much of 20th century art.

Flowering Apple Tree - circa 1920 - Oil on canvas, 100 x 78 cm - Brest, Musée Municipal. In this painting Bonnard seemed determined both to face up to a new problem with colour and to solve it. He succeeded in painting the delicate apple blossom against a glowing green background beyond the lattice of the gate at the front of the picture and, more difficult still, against the cerulean tones of the field. The subtle tones of the flowers seem to convey the joyful atmosphere of spring itself.

Landscape at Le Cannet. 1928 - Oil on canvas, 123 x 275 cm - Paris, M. and Mme Adrien Maeght's collection. In this painting Bonnard's landscape conforms to emotional rather than visual rules. Its field of vision is far wider than that of the human eye. The colours are striking, with the blue of the distant mountains, the orange roofs, the green foliage and the yellow and ochre foreground, in which there can be seen a mysterious figure.

THE PAINTER OF EVERYDAY LIFE

Most of Bonnard's paintings deal with everyday life. They consist of spontaneous images, depicting reality in its purest and simplest form, without unnecessary fiction. This was a reality grasped and drawn under the impulse of immediate sensations, to be recreated again and again through memory, forms and colour.

Bonnard's principal aim was to represent space in its entirety. It was not the subject which interested him - if by subject is meant something definite, historical or mythological. Rather, what obsessed him was the representation of the spaces in which modern man exists and events that may be neither exciting, moving nor epic: landscapes and gardens, breakfasts or naked figures in the bath, dogs and cats, fruit baskets, vases of flowers and kitchen utensils.

Bonnard had no wish to depict extraordinary events. As he said himself, his aim was to depict "What one sees on entering a room unexpectedly". He wanted to be able to seize onto the "infinitely near - this double proximity that is both psychological and optical and is a tremendous enigma. How can one paint this proximity? Painting is so rarely concerned with the representation of things that are close to us. On the contrary, its techniques have been developed to keep the world at a distance."

BONNARD AND HIS TIMES

	HIS LIFE AND WORKS	HISTORY	ART AND CULTURE
1867	Pierre Bonnard, son a civil servant, born 3 October at Fontenay-aux-Roses	Second Parliamentary Reform Bill passed Dominion of Canada established Hungary becomes separate kingdom	Edouard Manet: *The Execution Of The Emperor Maximilien* Death of Charles Baudelaire Renoir: *Lise With A Sunshade*
1887	Enrols in the Académie Julian	Foundation of the Indochinese Union Queen Victoria's Golden Jubilee	Van Gogh paints his series of *Sunflowers* Georges Seurat exhibits *The Grande Jatte* at the Salon of the XX in Brussels Giuseppe Verdi: *Otello*
1888	Graduates in law. Sérusier calls the group formed by his friends Bonnard, Ranson, Vuillard, Roussel, Maillol and Denis the Nabis	Cecil Rhodes acquires what becomes Rhodesia (Zimbabwe) Local Government Act sets up County Councils in England and Wales	Birth of T.S. Eliot Toulouse-Lautrec: *Bareback Rider at Fernando's*
1891	The great success of his poster France-Champagne encourages him to dedicate himself entirely to art. First exhibition by the Nabis	Michelin produces the first pneumatic tyres Creation of the Pangermanist Union signifies growing German nationalism	Death of Seurat and Rimbaud Thomas Hardy: *Tess Of The D'Urbevilles* Herman Melville: *Billy Budd*
1892	He exhibits seven pictures at the Salon des Indépendants	Financial scandal of the Panama Canal in France Expansion of the Belgian Congo	Oscar Wilde: *Lady Windermere's Fan* Rudyard Kipling: *Barrack Room Ballads* Paul Cézanne: *The Card Players*
1893	He sets up a studio in the Rue de Douai. He illustrates *Le Petit Solfège* of his brother-in-law Claude Terrasse	Bread riots in Sicily Gladstone introduces Second Home Rule Bill for Ireland, which is rejected by the House of Lords	Verdi: *Falstaff* W.B. Yeats: *The Rose* Oscar Wilde: *A Woman Of No Importance*
1894	He produces the poster in lithograph of *La Revue Blanche*. Meets Marie Boursin, alias Marthe de Meliny, who is 25	Opening of Manchester Ship Canal Beginning of the Sino-Japanese War The plague bacillus discovered	Claude Debussy: *L'Après-Midi D'Un Faune* Anthony Hope: *The Prisoner Of Zenda*
1898	He creates the marionettes for the Théâtre des Pantins of Franc-Nohain, which is banned by the censor. Nabis Exhibition at Vollard's	Battle of Omdurman: Kitchener defeats the Mahdi in Sudan Pierre and Marie Curie discover radium Death of Bismarck	Joseph Conrad: *Youth* H.G. Wells: *War Of The Worlds* Oscar Wilde: *Ballad Of Reading Gaol*
1900	He illustrates *Parallèlement* by Paul Verlaine	World Fair in Paris Dreyfus rehabilitated Boxer rising in China	Colette starts the Claudine series Gustav Klimt: *Philosophy* Alfred Jarry: *Ubu Enchained*

The use of orange and violet imbues Bonnard's painting with a unique sense of space and time. When the artist entered a room he behaved almost as though he was behind a camera. He assembled all the details necessary to describe objectively what he saw. He then selected a field of vision, bringing it into focus and choosing the figures and objects for his canvas.

The artist's attention was not limited to the concept of space. He also turned his attention to capturing the passing moment - which can never be repeated. His interest in a subject altered in accordance with the changing intensity of the light striking the images and creating colours of greater or lesser intensity.

His imagination was enthused by tiny details and routines which would have been viewed as mere insignificant encumbrances by many earlier painters. However, in the context of his absorbing reflections of everyday reality, they become vital witnesses of that particular instant.

Between 1925 and 1943 Bonnard took to making simple meteorological notes in his diary and these became the only sign of his reactions to events. Remarks such as "fine" or "cloudy" would be accompanied by a few sketches. Sometimes he used signs to allude to specific events.

1903	After the appearance at Vollard's of *Daphnis And Chloe*, illustrated by him, he exhibits in the Salon des Indépendants his *Portrait Of Claude Terrasse*. First exhibition at the Salon d'Automne with *Bourgeois Afternoon*	The Russian Social Democrat party splits into Bolsheviks and Mensheviks The Wright brothers make the first aeroplane flight Henry Ford founds the Ford Motor Company	Death of Paul Gauguin Henry James: *The Ambassadors* Bernard Shaw: *Man And Superman* Birth of Evelyn Waugh
1908	After travelling widely, he undertakes a series nude studies, of which *Nude Against The Light* is one. He illustrates *The-628-E8* of Octave Mirbeau	Formation of the Triple Entente (France, Great Britain and Russia) Asquith becomes Prime Minister The Austrians annex Bosnia	Henri Matisse: *Luxe* E.M. Forster: *Room With A View*
1910	Second consecutive year in the south of France which fascinates him	Death of Edward VII in England; George V succeeds him Japan annexes Korea Liberals win two General Elections in Britain over constitutional crisis	Igor Stravinsky: *The Firebird* E.M. Forster: *Howard's End* Fernand Léger: *Nudes In The Forest*
1912	He buys a little house near Vernon. His Paris studio is in the Rue Tourlaque	Balkans War flares up over partition of Turkish empire in Europe The *Titanic* sinks on its maiden voyage	Giorgio de Chirico: *Melancholy Of A Street* Ezra Pound: *Ripostes* Birth of Lawrence Durrell
1918	Elected Honourary President, with Renoir, of the group Young French Painting	Collapse of Germany and Austria Armistice ends First World War Creation of Yugoslavia and Czechoslovakia; civil war in Russia	Death of Apollinaire James Joyce: *Exiles* Lytton Strachey: *Eminent Victorians* Marcel Proust: *Young Girls In Flower*
1924	Has a great retrospective exhibition at the Drouet Gallery in Paris, with 68 pictures, (from *Girl With A Cat* of 1891 to *Vase Of Wild Poppies* of 1922)	Death of Lenin First Labour government in England with Ramsay Macdonald as Prime Minister	First Surrealist Manifesto by André Breton René Clair: *Entr'acte* Edwin Lutyens building New Delhi
1925	He buys a villa at Le Cannet in the south of France; he finally marries Marthe	Treaty of Locarno signed in London Hindenburg becomes president of Germany	Pablo Picasso: *The Dance* Virginia Woolf: *Mrs Dalloway* T.S. Eliot: *The Hollow Men*
1930	He exhibits seven canvases at the exhibition *Painting In Paris* at the Museum of Modern Art in New York. Illustrates *The Life Of Saint Monique* by Vollard	Airship R101 crashes near Calais, killing everyone on board First plastics manufactured	Death of D.H. Lawrence Salvador Dali and Luis Buñuel: *L'Age D'Or* T.S. Eliot: *Ash Wednesday* Birth of Ted Hughes
1942	Death of Marthe at Le Cannet.	Battles of El Alamein and Stalingrad Nazis implement their Final Solution to murder all Jews	Albert Camus: *The Outsider* Cesare Pavese: *The Beach*
1947	He dies in Le Cannet, 23 January	Marshall Aid to Europe inaugurated British quit India; India and Pakistan created Dutch leave Indonesia	Bertold Brecht: *Galileo* Jackson Pollock: *Full Fathom Five* Malcolm Lowry: *Under The Volcano*

On the day that Marthe died in 1942, he merely put a cross under the word "fine". His only recorded comment on the outbreak of World War II in 1939 - as big a public disaster as Marthe's death was a personal one - was the word "rainy". Each day that Bonnard described was different from the last. His sole aim was to link atmospheric movement to daily visual changes. Even though they were never identical, weather conditions often repeated themselves and were to be found filling his notebooks. Bonnard's real obsession was the need to recreate everything that lived and moved without losing anything. This was the essence of his painting, which tended to become an incessant search for "temps perdu" (time lost). He used forms that were still largely figurative (clearly recognisable objects).

The dazzling light in his canvases derived partly from Gauguin. He was also influenced by Van Gogh's revolutionary use of colour and the luminous images of Monet and Renoir. Yet, although he knew many of the famous revolutionaries of 20th century art, especially Matisse, he does not seem to have been much affected by their art. Instead, it seems to have been the revelation of the brilliantly strong, pure colours of the Mediterranean - that sea which he so much loved - which enthused him when painting either his alluring nudes or his dazzling landscapes.

THE WINDOW AND MIRROR

What is the first thing that we see on entering a room? Everything and nothing. Then, slowly, through memory, the image that seemed so hazy takes form on the canvas. In order to capture the moment in its entirety Bonnard often made use of two devices: the mirror and the window or glass door. These two elements became in some ways the emblems of his

paintings. The mirror reflects the room, revealing indiscriminately its objects and figures, and capturing unguarded poses. It shows that there can be no single point of view, and that no one perspective can take precedence over all others. The window works without mystery to open out the space between the interior and the external world. Both images extend and multiply ways of representation. They transcend the traditional limits between the outside and the inside. It was as though Bonnard understood that the future of painting was to be in ever-increasing artificiality - and in colour.

Henri Matisse, who was Bonnard's friend, was following a similar path but moving faster. He concentrated on the stylisation of outlines and on brilliant colour. Unlike Bonnard, Matisse was concerned with the decorative effect of his canvas. The minimal lines of his *Glass Door In Collioure* demonstrate the more abstract element in his work. Jean Clair said that Pierre Bonnard continued to organise "space in such a way that he succeeded in emptying the centre of the painting and filling the edges. In this way he produced a balanced and natural image, a spontaneous vision of the world."

Bonnard found inspiration in the work of much earlier painters. His first landscapes recall Jean-Baptiste-Camille Corot's harmonious canvases of the mid-19th century. His independent spirit was a legacy of his experiences with the Nabis group. Bonnard and Vuillard were from the start particularly close friends. At a creative level they understood each other perfectly. Besides Gauguin and Van Gogh, Monet and Renoir, Bonnard always admired Degas and Cézanne as well as the great Japanese print-makers; he also explored the new avenues that were being opened up by the use and development of photography. In this he showed himself once again

the direct heir of the great Impressionists, who had found that photography freed them from a formally posed view of the world.

THE REDISCOVERY OF FORM

Some time before 1920, Bonnard became dissatisfied with his work and radically revised it, returning to the study of drawing. In his own words: "Carried away by colour, almost unconsciously I had sacrificed form. However, form exists and it cannot be arbitrarily reduced or transposed. Consequently, I had to study drawing. After drawing it was composition, which must provide the balance. A painting that is well drawn is already half done."

Bonnard's rediscovery of the importance of drawing and design added a new solidity and form to his painting. This enabled it to weather each cultural shockwave that rolled out of Paris in the first third of the century. After the Fauvist exhibition in 1905, which heralded the true avant-garde of the new century, Parisian society turned to the Cubists around 1912 and then the Surrealists in the 1920s, pushing each new, increasingly unrealistic, school into the artistic limelight.

With tact and elegance, Bonnard corrected a defect in modern art. He managed to introduce a delightful element of intimacy into painting, without in any way compromising the monumental aspects of the Cubists. This was perhaps his greatest achievement.